IMAGES
of America

PETRIFIED FOREST
NATIONAL PARK

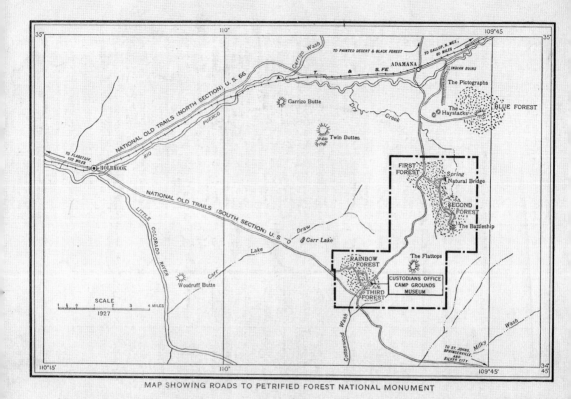

MAP SHOWING ROADS TO PETRIFIED FOREST NATIONAL MONUMENT

This 1927 map from *The Petrified National Monument, Arizona: Rules and Regulations* shows the 1911–1930 park boundary and the location of the major petrified wood accumulations in association with major roads and highways. The National Old Trails Road was the first cross-country highway, stretching from Baltimore, Maryland, to San Francisco, California. The northern branch, after realigning several miles north of the town of Adamana, later became part of Route 66. (National Park Service.)

ON THE COVER: Two tourists are enjoying the Old Faithful Log in the Rainbow Forest in the late 1920s. This log, considered to be the largest in the park, has long been a centerpiece of the petrified wood deposits. (National Park Service/Petrified Forest 24881.)

IMAGES
of America

PETRIFIED FOREST
NATIONAL PARK

William Gibson Parker

ARCADIA
PUBLISHING

Copyright © 2020 by William Gibson Parker
ISBN 978-1-4671-0490-6

Published by Arcadia Publishing
Charleston, South Carolina

Printed in the United States of America

Library of Congress Control Number: 2019952111

For all general information, please contact Arcadia Publishing:
Telephone 843-853-2070
Fax 843-853-0044
E-mail sales@arcadiapublishing.com
For customer service and orders:
Toll-Free 1-888-313-2665

Visit us on the Internet at www.arcadiapublishing.com

To the first superintendent, Charles J. "White Mountain" Smith, who turned an obscure national monument into a national park.

CONTENTS

ACKNOWLEDGMENTS

Quite a few people have made this book possible. Because it has been a national park unit for over 110 years, and visited for even longer, there is a very sizable number of historical images of the Petrified Forest to draw from. The park itself has a significant collection and I would like to thank the staff of Petrified Forest National Park, especially curator Matthew Smith, for the access. Khaleel Saba of the Western Archeological Conservation Center facilitated the return of the park photograph archive specifically for this project. John Muir and his daughter Helen extensively photographed their stay in Adamana in 1905 and 1906, and Virginia Bones, Isabel Ziegler, and Tom Leatherman at John Muir National Historic Site provided permission and also scans of select photographs from this collection. David Smith at the University of California Museum of Paleontology provided information and materials from the Camp and Alexander photograph collections. Michael Wurtz at the University of the Pacific oversees the Muir correspondence collection and allowed for use of some of their materials. The Petrified Forest is routinely contacted by families of men who served in the CCC at the park and who often donate photographs. I appreciate the donations of the Power, Holler, and LaVasseur families. Finally, I'd also like to thank the staff and editors at Arcadia Publishing, including Lindsey Givens, Stacia Bannerman, and Caitrin Cunningham for their assistance during the writing and publishing process.

National Park Service/Petrified Forest (NPS/PEFO) identifies photographs from the Petrified Forest collections. National Park Service/John Muir (NPS/JOMU) identifies photographs from the John Muir National Historic Site collections. The numbers sometimes paired with these abbreviations are catalog numbers.

INTRODUCTION

The petrified forests of Arizona have been a tourist attraction since the building of the railroad through Northern Arizona in the 1880s. Repeat photography has shown that, although the natural and cultural resources remain relatively unaltered, the park infrastructure has changed significantly, from trains and wagons at the turn of the last century to high-speed automobiles on the interstate highway. Traversed by major highways, an interstate, and the railroad, the Petrified Forest has always been a crossroads since prehistoric times as these modern routes follow much older trails.

The petrified wood deposits were first recorded by military expeditions following the 48th parallel; however, the oral traditions of indigenous peoples and archeological evidence show that the fossil forests had been of significance for over 10,000 years. Called Chalcedony Park in its earliest days, placer claims allowed for the mining and removal of the petrified wood. Alarmed local citizens were concerned about the rapid removal of the petrified wood by commercial entities, and how it would affect local tourism. In response, the Arizona territorial legislature set the area aside for protection in 1895, and although early attempts to designate the area as a national park failed, it was one of the first places set aside as a national monument under the Antiquities Act.

At the time of its establishment as a national monument in 1906, there were no buildings on-site, and only a few territorial wagon roads went through the "forests," as the wood accumulations were called. An old Mormon trail from St. Johns to Holbrook became part of the National Old Trails Road in 1919, passing through the southern end of the park, while a northern branch paralleled the train tracks, bringing much of the early automobile traffic.

Petrified Forest National Monument predates the creation of the National Park Service by a decade, and at first, the monument was under the direction of the US Lands Department out of Santa Fe. The initial custodians were stationed in the nearby railroad town of Adamana; essentially, they were whoever owned the Forest Hotel at the time. These custodians received $1 per month initially and were allowed rights to charge visitors for tours into the monument. They received direction from Frank Pinkley, who was the superintendent of Southwest monuments and was stationed at the Casa Grande monument. Of course, this allowed very little funding to make improvements much more than road grading, although one of the first custodians, Chester Campbell, put up a small wooden shade structure in the Second Forest.

The earliest significant buildings in the monument consisted of several tar paper shacks, built in the mid-1920s, which housed a museum and the custodian residence at Rainbow Forest. There was also the Rainbow Forest Lodge, a private enterprise providing food, gas, and curiosities to visitors. Two stone camping cabins were added to this business in the late 1920s.

The first on-site park superintendent, Charles J. "White Mountain" Smith, made significant improvements to these facilities starting in 1930. His staff designed and built roads, buildings, and trails. This included the Rainbow Forest complex with a stone headquarters building and ranger residences, the trail systems at Giant Logs, Long Logs, and Crystal Forest, and the main park road. Much of this work was accomplished using the Civilian Conservation Corps (CCC). Smith's layout and design are still utilized today and are a testament to his vision.

A large boundary expansion authorized by the Wilson administration in 1931 brought the Blue Forest and the Painted Desert areas into the park. This addition was critical because the northern route of the National Old Trails Road officially became part of the newly designated Route 66 in 1926 and the southern route, which ran close to the headquarters, was no longer a major travel route for tourists. Thus, it was important to tie into the Highway 66 traffic. Another longtime barrier had been the Puerco River, which when wet effectively cut off traffic to the forests from Adamana. The new area included the best place to construct a bridge across the river, and this was accomplished very shortly after the land was acquired.

This expansion had been proposed as early as 1907 when the Department of the Interior contacted John Muir for recommendations of key areas to add, and it was seen as a critical need for the push to elevate the monument to national park status. One of the main criticisms was that the Petrified Forest lacked significant scenic views and would never be worthy of a national park without them. The addition of the Painted Desert and its overlooks accomplished this goal. Indeed, this part of the monument had been one of Muir's favorite places, and he returned several times after 1906 with other notable conservationists, such as John Burroughs. Muir called the main overlook "Rustler's Roost."

Funding and visitation slowed during World War II, which also was the end of the CCC era, and by the mid-1950s, with increasing visitation through a new emphasis on travel and vacationing, the existing facilities were strained. The Mission 66 program created by NPS director Conrad Wirth provided relief, including a brand new visitors' center complex and housing along the newly established Interstate 40. National park status also was obtained during this time, accomplishing that long-sought goal.

The 2004 Petrified Forest Expansion Act doubled the size of the park to over 200,000 acres, and immediately, these areas proved their value in significant paleontological and archeological sites to be protected, as well as adding areas that provide increased opportunities for visitor recreation and activities. Long thought to be just for the protection of the largest deposit of petrified wood in the world, the Petrified Forest is globally significant and a leader in vertebrate paleontology, and its density and time range of archeology sites are changing views on the long history of human use and habitation in the area.

Primarily a science park, Petrified Forest has a long, exciting history as well as resources that rival those of any other park and justify its designation and protection as a national park.

One

CHALCEDONY PARK

Although long known and utilized by native peoples, the Petrified Forest was first historically documented in 1851 by the Sitgreaves Expedition. Two years later, the Whipple Expedition discovered the Black Forest while surveying the 35th parallel. Swiss geologist Jules Marcou determined that the wood likely was from the Triassic Period, and the scene was recorded by expedition artist Balduin Möllhausen with this woodcut in his *Diary of a Journey from the Mississippi to the Coasts of the Pacific*. (NPS/PEFO 24460.)

Chalcedony Park - Arizona Territory - (Adams & Shaw, Propriet...

Word of the "Forests of Stone" spread, and prospectors placed claims over the best areas. One such pair consisted of "Petrified" William Adams and S.L. Shaw, who in 1885 set up at what is now called Agate Mesa, christening the area "Chalcedony Park." Adams and Shaw sold the petrified wood and shipped out 18 tons worth by 1888. (NPS/PEFO 18810.)

Removal of the petrified wood prompted early conservation efforts. In 1885, the Arizona territorial legislature called on Congress to set the area aside as a national park. Early efforts were championed by Sen. John Fletcher Lacey, but all were unsuccessful. Lacey was an eight-term Republican senator from Iowa who wrote the Antiquities Act, which provides the president the ability to protect areas of scientific interest as national monuments. (NPS/PEFO 23509.)

Early visitors arrived by train and were taken by guides from Holbrook or Adamana through the various "forests," as the large accumulations of petrified wood were commonly called. They were named in the order they were reached, the First, Second, and Third Forests. Travel to the Third Forest required overnight camping. (NPS/PEFO 15845.)

A mother and her small children are pictured in the First Forest in 1903. The photograph is labeled "Agatized Ruins of a Great Primeval Forest Near Adamana, Arizona." Despite the apparent remoteness of the site, its proximity to the railroad made it easy to visit. (NPS/PEFO 34111.)

Rock formations such as Eagle Rock, named for the eagle's nest found on it, were destinations for the earliest explorers and visitors. Eagle Rock is an erosional rock pinnacle that was commonly photographed by early visitors and also featured in numerous postcards purchased to send back home. The site was in the First Forest, a prominent part of Chalcedony Park, until its collapse in 1940. Rock formations in the badlands enhanced the area's reputation as a place to see for the adventurous. Having one's photograph taken standing next to Eagle Rock was very common among visitors as well as the park rangers. (Above, NPS/PEFO 24504; left, NPS/PEFO 2822E1.)

Another prominent feature of Chalcedony Park was the natural bridge, a 100-foot-long petrified log that spans a gully. It was popular for early visitors to have their photograph taken on the log. In the late 1800s, a cowboy named John Paine won a $10 bet by successfully riding his horse across the log. (Henry Peabody, NPS/PEFO 18914.)

Afraid for the collapse of this popular feature, the Santa Fe Railway constructed support pillars underneath in 1911. The original pillars were replaced in 1917 by a steel-supported concrete beam, which is still at the site today. It is unclear how long this feature would have lasted without this support, as collapsed "bridges" are present in other parts of the park. (NPS/PEFO.)

Shortly after his arrival in 1895, rancher Adam Hanna supplemented his income by providing tours of Chalcedony Park. Hanna also served as the postmaster and brokered the removal of several train carloads of wood in 1899. Hanna was an opponent of early attempts to protect the area as a national park. The photograph above shows Hanna behind several large log pieces, probably in the First Forest, and the photograph below shows him perched on top of the Natural (Agate) Bridge in 1899. Hanna left the area in 1907 shortly after the monument was created. (Above, NPS/PEFO 24860; below, NPS/PEFO 2912.)

In 1898, the Santa Fe Railway built a railroad station north of the park. It was named Adamana, a contraction of Adam Hanna's name. Adamana would serve as the unofficial park headquarters until 1924. That the station name was an amalgamation of Hanna's first name with his wife, "Anna," is a longstanding, oft repeated, claim, but it is false. Mrs. Hanna's first name was actually Maggie. (NPS/PEFO 34559A.)

The Forest Hotel was constructed in Adamana in the late 1800s and served visitors for over 60 years. Hotel owners ran the livery service to the park, and after the establishment of the monument and for the next 18 years, whoever owned the hotel also served as the monument custodian. The hotel stayed in business until it burned in 1966. Here is a wagon set to depart from the hotel in 1895. (NPS/PEFO 15837.)

The most common place to visit was the First Forest, as it was the closest to Adamana. Besides Eagle Rock and the Natural Bridge, a sandstone feature known as the Snow Lady was a common destination. Unfortunately, this structure, like the Eagle Rock, was a victim of erosion and collapse in the 1950s. (NPS/PEFO 24506.)

This is a common petrified wood scene in the First Forest, with the subjects standing among the log sections; however, it is slightly unconventional in that only their heads are visible. The figures in the photograph are Adam Hanna and possibly his wife. They would have had to stand in that position for a while to compose this very early shot. (NPS/PEFO 2992.)

Cannon Rock, near the Natural Bridge, was a commonly visited log in Chalcedony Park. This feature is still mostly intact today but has mostly been forgotten because, as park infrastructure changed, some of the earlier popular features were not included along the new roads or trails. (George Grant, NPS/PEFO 18854.)

The Third, or Rainbow, Forest, located south of Chalcedony Park, was an overnight trip from Adamana because of the distance. The feature attraction here was a very large log termed by some the "Major Domo," shown here in 1900. This log was later named "Old Faithful" and is still a focal point of the park today. (NPS/PEFO 26067.)

Not all visitors came from the railroad. Territorial roads brought visitors in buggies from Holbrook. This 1899 photograph shows a well-dressed woman touring Rainbow Canyon, a large petrified wood site in the southern portion of the Rainbow Forest. This road is a spur off of the original Holbrook–Springerville road and is still wonderfully preserved today. The road went over the petrified wood deposit to keep wagons out of the muddy wash. The larger pieces of wood were moved to the side to line the road as a curb, and the petrified wood chips were rolled flat in the roadbed to create a paving. This type of road construction is unique, and the site is eligible for listing in the National Register of Historic Places. (NPS/PEFO 23510.)

Two

JOHN MUIR

Writer and conservationist John Muir came to Adamana in 1905 with his two daughters, Helen and Wanda. Helen had tuberculosis, and Muir and his daughters had just lost his wife and their mother, Wanda Louie, earlier that year. He hoped the dry desert air would cure all of their ills and looked forward to writing about his examinations of the giant petrified logs. No articles from Muir detail his time at Adamana, but the family took numerous photographs, creating an album of the trip. (NPS/JOMU 3268.179.)

RETURN IN 10 DAYS TO
FOREST HOTEL
AL. STEVENSON, Prop.,
ADAMANA · ARIZONA.

Mrs Mary Gillpatrick
Martinez
California

Muir and his daughters stayed at the Forest Hotel in Adamana. Stevenson family members were the proprietors and, surely, welcomed a personage such as Muir staying at their business. The Muirs took lots of photographs of the townspeople and local ranchers and must have been welcomed and accepted. This is an image of the complimentary stationery from the hotel used by Muir for much of his correspondence from the area. (NPS/JOMU 3592a.)

Marion & his guitar   Sept. '05

The Muir family's documentation of the town of Adamana is some of the best in existence. They photographed trains and townspeople. Unfortunately, they photographed more people than they did buildings, so the exact layout of the town remains a mystery. Muir seemed especially enthralled with Marion Stevenson, the young son of the hotel owners who appears in several photographs. Here is Marion with his guitar. (NPS/JOMU 3268.045.)

The Reo Mountaineer, getting ready

In the winter of 1905–1906, automobile pioneer Ransom Olds had just started the REO Motor Car Company, and to promote the new brand, he hired one of the best driver/mechanic teams in the country, Percy Megargel and David Fassett, to attempt a cross-country endurance run in a REO Mountaineer vehicle. It took 10 months to drive the 11,000 miles from New York to San Francisco and back. The trip was well covered by the media, and in remote places like Holbrook, Arizona, it was the first automobile townspeople had ever seen. The winter of 1905–1906 was particularly harsh, and driving east through Northern Arizona was miserable for the two men. They were lost in the snow in Flagstaff, blocked by Padre Canyon, and finally, when they reached Adamana in January 1906, the car was lost to quicksand in the Puerco River. Three weeks later, strong winter flows revealed the vehicle. It was pulled out, disassembled, cleaned, and rebuilt. Helen Muir's photograph captures the two men preparing the vehicle to depart. Megargel and Fassett completed their trip, arriving back in New York on June 12, to quite a celebration. (NPS/JOMU 3268.146.)

Hieroglyphics, Stork and Frog, Petrified Forest, Arizona

A common tourist attraction was the collection of pictographs near the Puerco River. These are actually petroglyphs, images pecked into a rock face using stone tools, as no paint was involved. According to local tribes, the petroglyphs throughout the park tell a story of the migration and activities of their ancestors who inhabited the Petrified Forest area in large numbers between 700 and 1,200 years ago. (NPS/PEFO.)

A popular early landmark in the area was "the Haystacks," two isolated mudrock hills named because they resembled stacks of hay to visitors approaching from Adamana. Names of features such as this are still used today, but their meaning is often lost on modern visitors driving by from a different angle and at a distance. (NPS/PEFO 15565.)

The eminent naturalist Muir was enthralled by the large petrified trees of the Petrified Forest and spent much of his time at Adamana exploring the forests. Here, Muir, Wanda, Helen, and a partner examine petrified log segments in the First Forest. This scene is little changed today, and the same pieces of wood viewed by Muir are in the same spots for modern visitors. (NPS/PEFO 24867.)

This photograph features petrified logs and rounds in the Black Forest, or the "Sigillaria Forest" as it was called by Muir. This area was outside and north of the original monument but was added in 1931. Today, it is a congressionally designated wilderness area. (NPS/PEFO 24862.)

Four miles east of Adamana is a set of badlands that Muir called the "South Badlands." Because of the blue colors of the rocks, Muir named the petrified wood assemblage there the Blue Forest, a name still used today. The Blue Forest also includes a series of preserved fossilized tree stumps, one being examined in this photograph by Muir and colleagues. (NPS/PEFO 24868.)

This photograph shows Muir on horseback in the Tepees area of the park, named for the rock formations that look like teepees. This area is known for deposits of fossil plants, including internal casts of giant horsetail plants. If Muir saw these, what he thought of them is unrecorded. (NPS/PEFO 24871.)

The Petrified Forest is high desert grassland and can be inhospitable for portions of the year, with a lack of standing water. Thus, early visitors needed to be opportunistic to get a drink. Such a scene was common for thousands of years but would seem strange, or even disgusting, to people today who are used to bottled drinks and indoor plumbing. The method used to capture a drink in the photograph below may seem a bit more "civilized" to modern senses. Muir is seen in this photograph kneeling next to a man scooping water with a cup. Many of the photographs have captions written in Muir's handwriting. (Right, NPS/JOMU 3268.066; below, NPS/JOMU 24866.)

John Muir made the first collection of fossil animals from the Petrified Forest, collecting bones from the Second and Black Forests. The majority of this collection went to his friend John C. Merriam at the University of California at Berkeley; however, Muir did keep at least one, the tooth of a phytosaurian reptile, which was later found in his home in Martinez, California. Muir also collected archeological artifacts from the Puerco Pueblo, which are also at his house. Muir's fossil collection came to the attention of Annie Montegue Alexander, who had founded the Museums of Paleontology and Zoology in Berkeley. On the basis of these finds, Alexander launched her own fossil expedition to the Petrified Forest in 1921. Her work at the forest ushered in several decades of paleontological work that is the foundation of the work still done today. (NPS/PEFO 24869.)

Pictured is a letter from John Muir to J.C. Merriam, dated December 15, 1906, telling him about the fossils he collected and offering to share them. Interestingly, there is no mention of the creation of Petrified Forest National Monument, which was created by proclamation nine days earlier, suggesting that Muir may not have known about it yet. The earthquake mentioned in the letter was the Great San Francisco Earthquake of 1906. Muir was at Adamana when the earthquake happened and was notified by telegram (shown below). He left immediately to examine damage to his home and did not return to the Petrified Forest again that year, although in the next decade he made several more trips to the area. (Both, Courtesy of John Muir Papers, Holt-Atherton Special Collections, University of the Pacific Library. © 1984 Muir-Hanna Trust.)

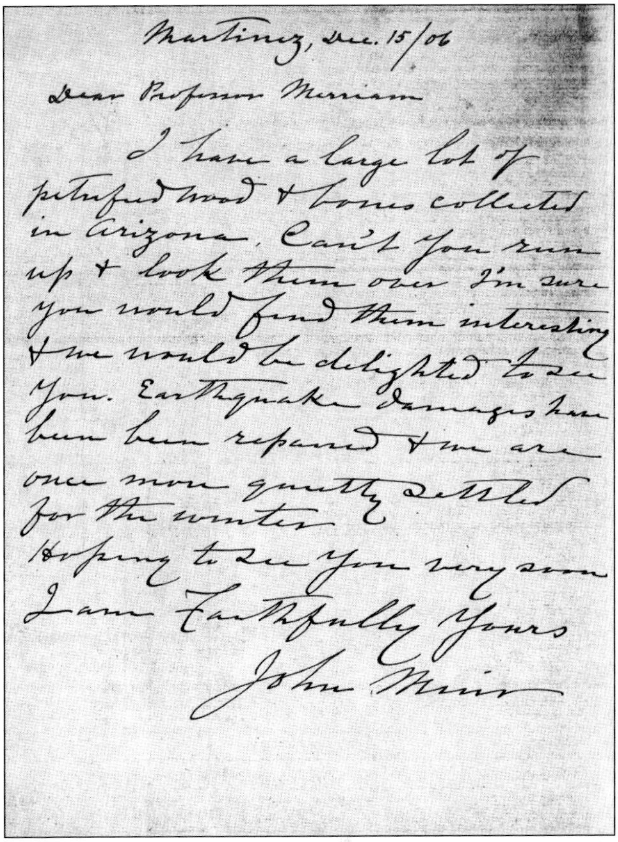

Martinez, Dec. 15/06

Dear Professor Merriam

I have a large lot of petrified wood & bones collected in Arizona. Can't you run up & look them over I'm sure you would find them interesting & we would be delighted to see you. Earthquake damages here have been repaired & we are once more quietly settled for the winter

Hoping to see you very soon I am Faithfully Yours

John Muir

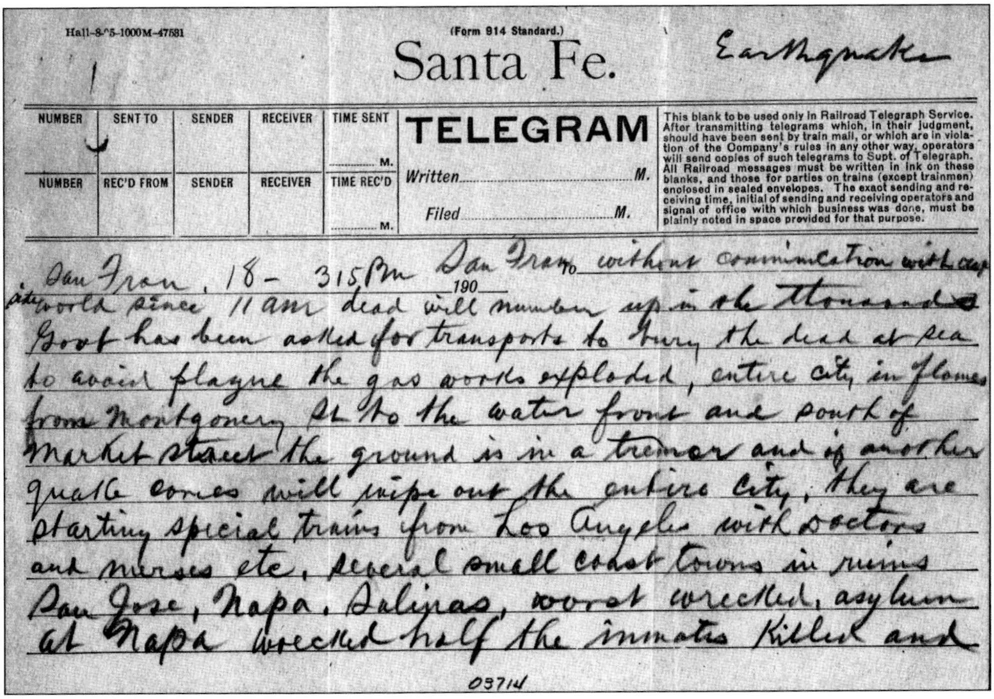

Hall-8-^5-1000M-47581

(Form 914 Standard.)

Santa Fe.   Earthquake

TELEGRAM

NUMBER	SENT TO	SENDER	RECEIVER	TIME SENT		
					M.	
NUMBER	REC'D FROM	SENDER	RECEIVER	TIME REC'D		
					M.	

Written _____ M.

Filed _____ M.

This blank to be used only in Railroad Telegraph Service. After transmitting telegrams which, in their judgment, should have been sent by train mail, or which are in violation of the Company's rules in any other way, operators will send copies of such telegrams to Supt. of Telegraph. All Railroad messages must be written in ink on these blanks, and those for parties on trains (except trainmen) enclosed in sealed envelopes. The exact sending and receiving time, initial of sending and receiving operators and signal of office with which business was done, must be plainly noted in space provided for that purpose.

San Fran, 18 — 315 Pm San Fran without communication with outer world since 11 am dead will number up in the thousands Govt has been asked for transports to bury the dead at sea to avoid plague the gas works exploded, entire city in flames from Montgomery St to the water front and south of Market street the ground is in a tremor and if another quake comes will wipe out the entire city, they are starting special trains from Los Angeles with doctors and nurses etc, several small coast towns in ruins San Jose, Napa, Salinas, worst wrecked, asylum at Napa wrecked half the inmates killed and

03714

27

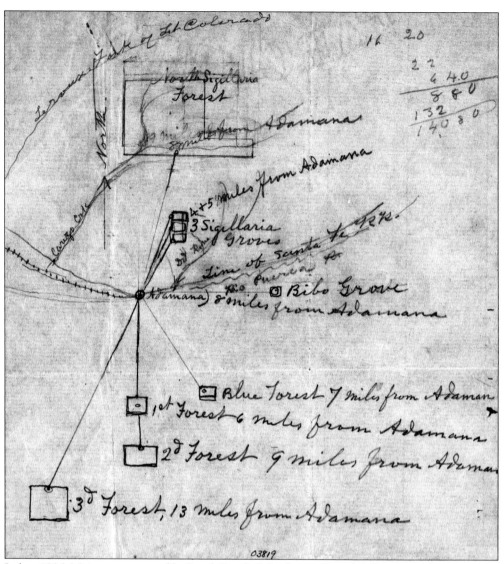

In late 1906, Muir was contacted by Frank Bond of the General Land Office in Washington, DC, about the locations of the largest petrified wood deposits in the Petrified Forest area. Despite just being established a month earlier, this correspondence shows that the government was already interested in expanding the monument. On January 15, 1907, Muir sent Bond this sketch showing the locations of the forests and other major features. Muir has often been given credit for the establishment of Petrified Forest as a national monument; however, there is presently no documentation that shows that Muir had anything to do with the creation of the monument. For several years after his correspondence with Bond, Muir repeatedly told friends that the Petrified Forest would be expanded at his suggestion. Unfortunately, when the Blue and Black Forests were finally added in 1931, that expansion also had nothing to do with Muir. To date, there is no landmark in the park named for Muir. (John Muir Papers, Holt-Atherton Special Collections, University of the Pacific Library. © 1984 Muir-Hanna Trust.)

Three

EARLY CUSTODIANS AND TOURISTS

By 1906, Iowa representative John Fletcher Lacey and others had been unsuccessful in passing legislation to create Petrified Forest National Park, so they tried a different, more successful tactic. Sponsored by Lacey, the Antiquities Act of 1906 gave the president of the United States the power to set aside areas of scientific interest as national monuments. On December 8, 1906, Pres. Theodore Roosevelt used the Antiquities Act to establish the Petrified Forest National Monument. (Library of Congress.)

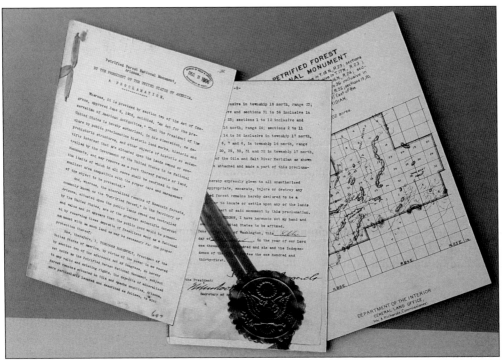

The proclamation by President Roosevelt states that "preserving the remnants of the Mesozoic Forest" would serve the common good and be of scientific interest. Thus, Petrified Forest became the first area in the United States to be protected because of fossils. (NPS/PEFO.)

Whoever owned the Forest Hotel was hired to be the monument custodian. The first was Al Stevenson, a Scandinavian immigrant who ran the hotel with his wife and children. Stevenson also provided livery service to the main attractions of the monument, including the three forests and archeological sites, like the Puerco Pueblo and the petroglyphs. This photograph shows the Stevenson home in Adamana. (King Collection, NPS/PEFO 34559A.)

In 1902, the King family from Chicago visited the forests. They later sent the Stevensons copies from their trip photo album. Here is the family picnicking. Scenes like this would have been very common when visitors used the old territorial roads and there were no restaurants or gift shops in the monument yet. (King Collection, NPS/PEFO.)

This 1910 photograph shows early visitors to the Second Forest. Originally, a series of roads ran through all of the petrified wood deposits. Most of these were removed by the early 1930s, and in many places, the old road was turned into part of the current trail system. (Author's collection.)

Pictured is a group of men standing on either side of the Natural Bridge around 1912. Note the stone supports placed under the bridge in 1911 by the railroad. At this time, many of the major features of the monument, such as the Natural Bridge, were on private land not owned by the US government. This caused issues in the early management of the area because the monument

did not have control of some of its major features that it was designated to protect. In the late 1920s, legislation was passed by Congress that allowed for the exchange of these lands for federal property elsewhere. (Library of Congress.)

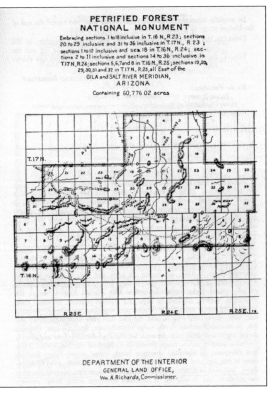

PETRIFIED FOREST
NATIONAL MONUMENT

Embracing sections 1 to 18 inclusive in T. 16 N., R.23; sections
20 to 29 inclusive and 31 to 36 inclusive in T.17 N., R 23 ;
sections 1 to 12 inclusive and sec. 18 in T.16 N., R.24; sections 2 to 11 inclusive and sections 14 to 36 inclusive in
T.17 N.,R.24; sections 5,6,7and 8 in T.16 N., R.25 ; sections 13,20,
29,30,31 and 32 in T.17 N., R.25, all East of the
GILA and SALT RIVER MERIDIAN,
ARIZONA

Containing 60,776 02 acres

T.17 N.

T.16 N.

R 23 E.   R 24 E.   R 25 E.

DEPARTMENT OF THE INTERIOR
GENERAL LAND OFFICE,
Wm. A. Richards, Commissioner.

In 1911, Pres. William H. Taft reduced the size of the monument from 60,776 acres (left) to 25,626 acres (below), following the recommendations of George P. Merrill of the US National Museum. Merrill had been sent to survey the monument because of concerns that the original designated area included too much land outside of the petrified wood deposits against the wording of the Antiquities Act. This action represents the first time the Antiquities Act was used to reduce the size of a monument. The 2004 Expansion Act included some of these areas removed in 1911. (Both, NPS/PEFO.)

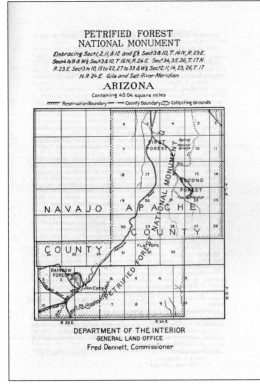

PETRIFIED FOREST
NATIONAL MONUMENT

Embracing Sec.1, 2, 11, & 12 and E½ Sec.3 & 10, T. 16 N, R. 23 E.
Sec.4 to 9 & W½ Sec.3 & 10, T 16 N, R.24 E   Sec.34, 35, 36, T.17 N.
R.23 E   Sec.3 to 10, 15 to 22, 27 to 33 & W½ Sec.2, 11, 14, 23, 26, T 17
N. R. 24 E   Gila and Salt River Meridian
ARIZONA

Containing 40.04 square miles

Reservation Boundary   County Boundary   Collecting Grounds

NAVAJO   APACHE

COUNTY   COUNTY

DEPARTMENT OF THE INTERIOR
GENERAL LAND OFFICE
Fred Dennett, Commissioner

In 1913, Chester B. Campbell took over the operation of the Forest Hotel and became the second custodian of the monument. Campbell also ran the livery and made road improvements. This 1914 photograph shows him leading a wagon team to begin a trip to the forests. (NPS/PEFO 29527.)

Campbell made many improvements to the monument, including minor wash crossings and upgraded roads. He also built a wooden shade structure in the Second Forest for visitor use, as seen in this photograph from 1916. (Grace Ireland Collection, NPS/PEFO.)

This photograph, taken a year before the crossbeam was constructed, shows a better view of Agate Bridge with the original stone pillars. These pillars were dismantled and removed prior to the crossbeam being installed. Unfortunately, no photographs are known of this work being done. (Grace Ireland Collection, NPS/PEFO.)

In 1916, the National Park Service was formally established, with Stephen T. Mather as the first director. Petrified Forest National Monument was included in this fledgling organization. Here is Mather sitting on a log in the Third Forest during a 1923 visit. (NPS/PEFO 18725.)

Chester Campbell left Adamana in 1918, moving to Holbrook to open Campbell's Coffee House, an early landmark known for its spicy chili. Succeeding Campbell were William "Petrified Bill" Nelson and his wife, Lucy. While Lucy ran the hotel, Bill Nelson dedicated himself to protecting the forest. In several cases, he chased down visitors on a motorcycle and made them drop pieces of petrified wood while looking down the barrel of his Winchester rifle. (Lucy Nelson Collection, NPS/PEFO 24712.)

At first, Nelson lived in the old shade house in the Second Forest, but in 1924, he moved down to the Rainbow Forest and set up a museum for visitors close to the edge of Jim Camp Wash. Note the "Old Faithful" log on the horizon in the distance. The writing across the top reads, "Mrs. Livingston." (NPS/PEFO.)

This 1924 photograph shows the interior of the first museum. Nelson collected petrified wood specimens for display and painstakingly made thin sections of the wood and lantern slides for presentations. (NPS/PEFO 34098.)

An early campground was added at Rainbow Forest around 1926. The Rainbow Forest had a campground in various spots until the 1950s, when it was closed. Afterwards, the park was without a campground for more than 70 years. (NPS/PEFO 24297.)

Joe Carmac,   Geo. W. P. Hunt,   William Melson
etrified Forest, July 1?, 1924

One prominent early visitor was the first governor of Arizona, which became a state in 1912, George W.P. Hunt. Called the "Old Walrus," Hunt was known for his size, drooping mustache, and style of dress. He was governor of Arizona several times, 1912–1919, 1923–1929, and 1931–1933. He also served as the US minister to Siam (now Thailand) in 1920. Hunt died in 1934 and is buried in Papago Park, which originally was a national monument, in Phoenix, where his pyramidal tomb is a local landmark. This 1924 photograph shows Hunt (center) and a guest with William Nelson (right) in the Rainbow Forest. (NPS/PEFO 34098.)

Adamana businessman Homer "Uncle Dick" Grigsby established the Rainbow Forest Lodge in 1928. Built of native stone, Grigsby included a lunch counter, curio shop, gas station, and later, camping cabins. Shown here shortly after construction, the building still stands today and serves as a gift shop for the Ortega National Parks company. (NPS/PEFO 24950.)

An ex-cowboy with the notorious Hashknife outfit, Grigsby ran the lodge until the 1950s. He passed away in 1965 at the age of 96 and is buried in the Holbrook Cemetery. Because of his long association with the lodge, he features prominently in much of the early history of the monument. He also collected and shared fossils with paleontologists working in the area and has a fossil plant (*Lyssoxylon grisgbyi*) named after him. (Strickland Collection, NPS/PEFO.)

Grigsby's lodge and Nelson's museum served as the monument center for years. Eventually, Grigsby added a set of camping cabins to his business, and as more monument staff were hired, several residences were added to the area, which served as the park headquarters until 1962. (NPS/PEFO 15730.)

Here is another view of the early National Park Service buildings, which were collectively known as the "Tarpaper Shacks." These served as an early museum, visitors' center, and housing for the rangers. (George Grant, NPS/PEFO.)

Meanwhile, north of the monument on the rim of the Painted Desert, Herbert Lore was constructing a new business close to the road that would soon be designated Route 66. Lore would call his building the Stone Tree House, and later the Painted Desert Inn. This is the only known photograph of that early construction phase in 1924. (NPS/PEFO 26238.)

By 1927, Petrified Forest had been a monument for 21 years and part of the National Park Service for 11. This is the cover of the national monument's rules and regulations, printed in 1927. (Author's collection.)

Norman Macleod was custodian from 1927 to 1928. Building a mock campfire from pieces of petrified wood at Agate Bridge are Macleod (right) and a couple of Boy Scouts. Macleod later became a well-known poet and novelist. (NPS/PEFO 24713.)

A very early focus of the monument custodians was keeping a steadily increasing number of visitors from absconding with pieces of petrified wood. By 1928, annual visitation was at 75,000 people. This early photograph shows a mock confrontation between "ranger and visitor." (Harold Meyer Collection, NPS/PEFO 34098.)

Another significant issue facing the monument was the Puerco River. Although dry most of the year, when it was wet, it would seriously affect visitors. This was amplified by the fact that the main highway through the area, Route 66, was located north of the river. These 1929 photographs show a wagon team and passengers crossing a wet river south to get back to Adamana. When the river flowed from the summer monsoon rains, it was impassible. A bridge was needed, but the best construction area was not part of the monument. (Above, Dudley Scott Collection, NPS/PEFO 5006; left, Dudley Scott Collection, NPS/PEFO 5011.)

Four

THE FIRST
SUPERINTENDENT

In 1928, it was clear to regional superintendent Frank Pinkley that the Petrified Forest needed a more experienced custodian to deal with increasing visitation and the lack of infrastructure. His choice was Charles J. "White Mountain" Smith. A Connecticut Yankee, Smith was chief ranger at the Grand Canyon and had gotten his start as a stagecoach driver at Yellowstone. Smith arrived as a custodian, but in 1932, he was promoted to full-time superintendent. He stayed in this position until 1940, and the work accomplished under his administration still serves as the infrastructure base in use by staff and visitors today. (NPS/PEFO 18685.)

White Mountain Smith (left) is pictured in front of the original museum building in the late 1920s with an early visitor. These buildings were described as dilapidated tar paper shacks, not worthy of a national monument headquarters. Soon after his arrival, Smith started looking at replacing these buildings with a nicer, stone construction headquarters building. (NPS/PEFO 24721.)

Dama Margaret Smith met White Mountain while they worked at the Grand Canyon, and they were married shortly afterwards. Dama Smith was a talented writer who documented their time at Grand Canyon in the book *I Married a Ranger*. Shortly after their arrival at the Petrified Forest, she wrote a new guidebook for the monument. (Author's collection.)

In the Rainbow Forest where the headquarters was situated, the primary feature was a petrified log of immense size. It was very popular with visitors, and Dama Smith dubbed it "Old Faithful." Her rationale behind the name was that this log was to Petrified Forest what the Old Faithful geyser was to Yellowstone. That name is still used today. Note the original territorial road that ran by the base of the tree and today is now part of the Giant Logs Trail. (NPS/PEFO 14636.)

Mrs. Cammerer

Another very common attraction for early visitors was the abandoned pueblo just south of the Puerco River and its associated petroglyphs. Although it had been recommended by John Muir for inclusion in 1907, this attraction was still outside of the monument in the late 1920s. This 1930 photograph shows National Park Service deputy director Arno Cammerer's wife, Ida, enjoying the petroglyphs at the site. (NPS/PEFO 15838.)

Custodian Smith worked tirelessly with the National Park Service to obtain some of the main features of the monument, such as Agate Bridge, that were on private land at that point. In 1930, Congress authorized the NPS to do land exchanges, and these private parcels were acquired adding not only Agate Bridge but also the First Forest. The stage was set to start developing these features for increased visitation. This early photograph shows the gates at the road entrance to the First Forest. (NPS/PEFO 15673.)

Two prominent visitors were Albert Einstein and his wife, Elsa, who toured the monument on March 31, 1931, during their second visit to the United States. Reportedly, Einstein was enthralled by the site of the petrified wood and asked many questions. This photograph shows Einstein standing (front, fourth from left) next to White Mountain Smith in front of the museum building. (NPS/PEFO 23648.)

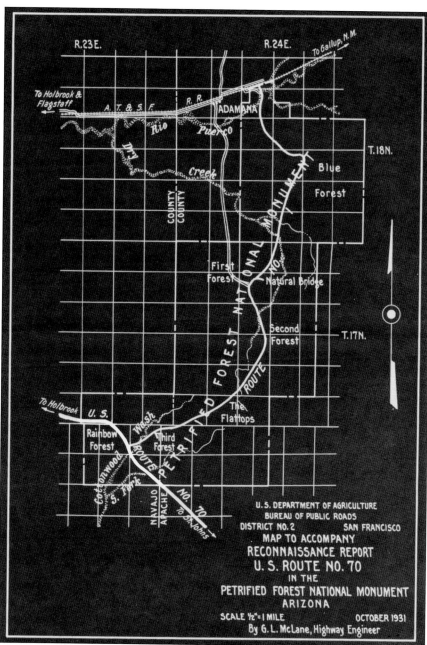

In 1931, Pres. Woodrow Wilson signed legislation that significantly expanded the monument, adding the Blue Forest and Painted Desert sections. One of the first goals was to develop an all-weather road for tourists, as the existing roads were prone to flooding and erosion. Furthermore, they were not continuous to all of the popular locations. The proposed new route stretched from Highway 70 to the south (the National Old Trails Road) to Adamana in the north. The route was designed to pass by key features of the monument, including the First, Second, and Third Forests; Agate Bridge; the Blue Forest; and Puerco Pueblo. This map from 1931 accompanied the reconnaissance report for the new road. Reportedly, White Mountain Smith scouted the route personally on horseback. (NPS/PEFO.)

Initially, the road was graveled with dip crossings across the major washes, notably Dry Wash. Nonetheless, it was a significant improvement over the old territorial roads, which were nothing more than old wagon roads that flooded and were often impassible after wet weather. The new road was the first to be planned and built for the automobile, which by this time had become the dominant mode of travel for Americans. This early photograph shows the road through the portion of the monument south of Highway 66. (NPS/PEFO 18861.)

This image shows how the 1932 road reconnaissance was done pre-GPS or satellite photograph, driving a vehicle across the grassland, taking periodic photographs, and marking them with a pen. This spot is looking to the north to eventually connect with Highway 66. (NPS/PEFO.)

By 1931, the tar paper shacks were no longer appropriate, and work was started on a new stone headquarters building. The contract was awarded to Phoenix contractor Del Webb. Webb's company would go on to become one of the largest developers in the Phoenix area. In this 1931 photograph, the construction of what is now the Rainbow Forest Museum is underway. Additional work included leveling the area around the building for parking and access. (NPS/PEFO 25904.)

The finished building had four rooms, a central museum space for visitors, two side office areas for staff, and a cellar. A large plaza in front provided parking and access, and a trail exited from the back of the building into the Giant Logs area of the Rainbow Forest, including the Old Faithful petrified log. This building would serve as the park headquarters until 1962 and is still a visitors' center today. (NPS/PEFO 24981.)

The main room housed the park museum, where visitors could see and learn about some of the Triassic fossils, as well as the petrified wood, found in the park. Navajo blankets adorned the walls, and there was also a mineral exhibit. A prominent feature was an overhead skylight that provided natural light. The floor was stamped red concrete that was glazed and polished. The people in the photograph below are Dama Smith and ranger Frank Winess. Winess served as chief ranger of the park for more than two decades. He was known as the "singing ranger" and spent a short time trying to make movies in Hollywood. (Above, NPS/PEFO 15764; below, NPS/PEFO 15766.)

AUG. 29 -'31   P.F. ROAD - UNDISTURBED WOOD   1208

New construction in the headquarters area in the Rainbow Forest included not only the headquarters and museum building, but also housing for employees, a garage, and storage buildings. New roads and parking lots, as well as a trail network through the Giant Logs area, were built to provide visitors a closer experience with the petrified wood. A rectangular parking area served as the approach to the buildings from the north over the Jim Camp Wash. The photograph above shows stone buildings under construction, with tents for the workers. A final addition was a campground in 1934, shown below. (Above, NPS/PEFO 24969; below, NPS/PEFO 24965.)

Past visitors were hampered by poor roads and a lack of bridge crossings. After the main road was constructed, the monument worked on building bridges. The southernmost bridge, crossing Dry Wash, was built by a private contractor in 1931. The bridge deck has been replaced several times through the years, most recently in 2020, but the original lower stonework still remains. The rest of the Dry Wash crossings consisted of simple dip crossings, which were replaced by box culverts in 1934. These were also fully replaced in 2020. (Above, NPS/PEFO 23653; below, NPS/PEFO 23652.)

However, the most needed and most significant bridge constructed under Superintendent Smith was the one spanning the Puerco River. Once impassable during wet weather, the north and south portions of the park were now traversable year-round. The photograph above shows the bridge under construction in 1932; below is the completed span. This bridge was later listed in the National Register of Historic Places; however, it was in poor condition in the early 1990s and was replaced by the current bridge. Unfortunately, the original bridge was demolished. (Both, Library of Congress.)

The dedication of the Puerco River Bridge was a huge affair with many local citizens; dignitaries, such as Gov. George W.P. Hunt; National Park Service officials, like Director Horace Albright; and even a marching band turning out. The following day, Albright went down to the Rainbow Forest to dedicate a memorial plaque for NPS founder Stephen T. Mather. The plaque is on the Giant Logs Trail at Rainbow Forest and is the only one personally dedicated by Albright. (Both, Library of Congress.)

The bridging of the Puerco River allowed year-round continuous travel from the south end of the monument up to the Painted Desert portion. A new road to the northern section was scouted out to tie in with Route 66, the main east-west highway designated in 1926. This photograph is from the original survey, showing the proposed route intersecting Highway 66. From there, the road went north to the Painted Desert overlooks and the Painted Desert Inn, eventually intersecting the eastern portion of Route 66. (NPS/PEFO.)

Acquisition of the Blue Forest area added Puerco Pueblo. A checking station was added for southbound traffic coming from Adamana and Route 66. A comfort station was also added at Agate Bridge (pictured). The trail from the parking area to Agate Bridge originally passed through the center of the structure. The center portion was closed in the 1970s; however, it was restored to its original look in 2016. (NPS/PEFO 15615.)

Another addition in 1931 was the Painted Desert section to the north. This area was served by Herbert Lore's Stone Tree House. This building provided limited lodging, food, and drinks for travelers. Constructed of native stone as well as petrified wood from the Black Forest, the building was purchased by the National Park Service in 1936. This 1932 photograph shows the proposed route of the new Painted Desert Rim Drive past the lobby entrance of the building. (NPS/PEFO.)

Other sites were developed to improve the visitor experience. In the Rainbow Forest was the foundation of a collapsed pueblo that had originally been constructed from petrified wood. After a detailed archeological investigation, the structure was rebuilt as an exhibit. Agate House can still be visited today and is listed in the National Register of Historic Places. This photograph shows the cleared foundation and the beginning of reconstruction work. (NPS/PEFO 25845.)

This 1934 photograph, taken by eminent National Park Service photographer George Grant, shows the Agate House as completed. This structure is still a popular attraction today with those willing to make the long trek on the Long Logs Trail. Grant served as the first chief photographer for the park service, and although relatively unknown by name, his national park photography work has been seen by millions. Another 1934 George Grant photograph (below) shows a young couple in the Giant Logs area. The Old Faithful log is visible to the left on the other side of the trail. (Above, NPS/PEFO 24285; below, NPS/PEFO 24878.)

By the middle of 1934, the park headquarters was starting to take shape, and this scene is still familiar today. The main parking lot is completed, flanked by Grigsby's Rainbow Forest Lodge and the Petrified Forest headquarters building and museum. The Giant Logs Trail, as well as the main park road, has been constructed, and the Jim Camp Wash has been bridged. The old tar paper shacks were still being used in part as residences, but that was about to change with the next phase of park construction. Future construction would be done by a new national program called the Works Progress Administration and the associated Civilian Conservation Corps. The photograph at left shows the original view of the Giant Logs Trail from the back of the museum. (Both, NPS/PEFO.)

Five

THE CIVILIAN CONSERVATION CORPS

Pres. Franklin Delano Roosevelt came into office during the Great Depression and very quickly launched his signature New Deal program, which provided funding to put unemployed men across the country to work. Many of these projects took place in national parks and monuments, and Petrified Forest was no exception. The first group of Civilian Conservation Corps enrollees for Petrified Forest arrived on July 3, 1934, and were stationed in tents along the Puerco River. (NPS/PEFO 24402.)

This photograph shows an early group of enrollees in 1934. Note the German shepherd dog to the left; also, one of the enrollees is holding a puppy at right center, showing that the men had pets and mascots. There is a variety of clothing styles. The enrollees are wearing standard uniforms, members of the cooking staff are identifiable on the left, older men who served as teachers and supervisors are in plain clothes, and there are several men in military uniforms. A number of

enrollees are African American because the CCC, unlike the military, was not segregated; this was achieved mainly through the efforts of Illinois representative Oscar DePriest, who insisted that the enabling legislation ban discrimination based on "race, color, or creed." (Power Collection, NPS/PEFO.)

The earliest CCC projects consisted of constructing spur roads off of the main park road to places like the First (Jasper) and Blue Forests, and also trail work such as the Second (Crystal) Forest loop trail and the trail to Newspaper Rock. Workers also constructed the upper Blue Forest loop, which is still used today, and built a connecting trail through the badlands of the Blue Forest. These photographs show culvert building in the Third Forest and construction of the Blue Forest Trail. The majority of the CCC construction is still used today, a testament to their skill and hard work. (Above, NPS/PEFO 15954; below, NPS/PEFO 15773.)

Within a few months, the workers were moved to more permanent barracks in the Rainbow Forest area, located closer to the park headquarters. This served as their base of operations for several years. The photograph above shows this camp from a distance, and at right is work on the nearby Petroglyph Canyon Trail. This early work was designed to allow visitors to see most of the park's important natural and cultural resources, including petrified wood, badland exposures, and archeological sites. Unfortunately, many of these trails were closed in the 1950s and 1960s. (Both, NPS/PEFO 15652.)

An early CCC worker at Petrified Forest was Michael Strank, a Slovakian immigrant from Pennsylvania who served for 18th months. Strank later joined the Marine Corps and served with distinction as a sergeant. He is famous for being one of the six men in the second flag raising on Iwo Jima during World War II that was immortalized in the Rosenthal photograph, and was the leader of the squad specifically chosen for the task. Unfortunately, Strank was killed by friendly fire a couple of days later. He did not have to endure some of the ordeals the other team members faced when they returned home. He is a major character in the book and movie *Flags of Our Fathers*. Never a naturalized US citizen, Strank was made an honorary citizen in 2008. He exemplifies the contributions immigrants have made to the country. (US Marine Corps.)

An important project undertaken by the CCC at Petrified Forest was the construction of a 16-mile-long water line to bring water from the Puerco River down to the park headquarters at Rainbow Forest, where attempts to drill a well had been unsuccessful. The majority of the work was done by hand; however, in some places, the rock was so hard that steam shovels and dynamite were used. In a couple of places, the pipe was laid above ground and then buried. This is still the longest hand-dug CCC waterline in the National Park Service, and was still in use until 2016, when it was bypassed and replaced. (Above, NPS/PEFO 15998; right, NPS/PEFO 15996.)

CIVILIAN CONSERVATION CORPS

U. C. 646841

Unit **Certificate**

THIS CERTIFIES THAT ___Paul LeVasseur___ of
Company ___3342___ has satisfactorily completed ___15___
hours of instruction in ___First Aid___ and
is therefore granted this Certificate.

Harold W. Cole
Project Superintendent.

James T. Frantz Jr
Company Commander.

Hubert N. Clark
Camp Educational Adviser.

Date ___Dec. 5, 1940___ Place ___Adamana, Arizona___

GPO   6—9671

The Civilian Conservation Corps was important not only for the work completed and pay received—all but $5 each month went back to the men's families—but also for the training and education earned. One of the major goals of the program was to build a skilled workforce, and this came in handy later during World War II. This is an enrollee's first aid training certificate. (LeVasseur Collection, NPS/PEFO.)

The CCC provided training not only for manual labor but also for skills such as cooking, typing, and art. Petrified Forest workers excavated, cleaned fossils, and gave presentations to visitors, among a variety of duties. Camps had newsletters to keep enrollees informed, and creation of these newsletters was also one of the available duties. This publication was called the *Forest Desert* and was produced in 1939. (NPS/PEFO 5193-1A-1.)

Other activities included a CCC rodeo, held at the Navajo County Fairgrounds in nearby Holbrook. The fairgrounds included a dirt track, and this photograph shows CCC workers racing horses as part of the rodeo competition. (Holler Collection, NPS/PEFO.)

Men were assigned to work groups and became fast friends with those in their group, as well as in their barracks. Many of the photographs of enrollees show them in these work groups and often provide the names and nicknames of their friends and coworkers. This image shows the "stone mason gang" with "Popeye" on the right. (NPS/PEFO 24174.)

The final CCC camp was located to the north, near the Puerco River. This move accommodated a shift in work priorities from the southern end of the park to the northern end, and moving the camp shortened the commute. Most of these boys were from Pennsylvania, and the final group was from Scranton. The picture below shows some of the men posing outside of their barracks. Many workers were from lower-income families and tough working-class neighborhoods, and this background is captured superbly in their facial expressions and body language. The inscription reads, "The Gang by Barracks 4." (Above, NPS/PEFO; below, NPS/PEFO 24184.)

The photograph above shows another group installing a water tank on the rim of the Painted Desert. Despite the hard labor, these boys all look happy, and the sense of camaraderie is strong. Below is a similar scene of exuberance with a large work crew leaving a site at the end of the day to return to camp. Many of these men had never been west of the Mississippi River and were learning new skills that would come to serve them well. It must have been quite the adventure to have a job, support one's family, see new places, and make new friends. CCC photograph collections commonly record these long-lasting friendships. (Above, LaVasseur Collection, NPS/PEFO 5192-2A; below, NPS/PEFO 20702B.)

One of the largest CCC projects in the monument was the remodel of the Painted Desert Inn. Originally the Stone Tree House (shown above in 1932), owned by Hebert Lore and acquired by the park service in 1936, the building was determined to be unstable and not of an appropriate architectural design. Under the guidance of NPS architect Lawrence Skidmore, the building was redesigned in the Pueblo Revival style. All of the restoration work was done by the CCC. This building still stands today and is now a national historic landmark. The photograph below shows the crew during the early portion of the work. (Above, NPS/PEFO 26211; below, NPS/PEFO 26206.)

Unstable foundations and walls were replaced, and numerous rooms were added to the building, including restrooms and six sleeping rooms. Decor included hand-painted skylights and tin light fixtures. This photograph shows the construction of stone steps on the east side of the building. (NPS/PEFO 26196.)

All of the walls are constructed from native stone. Pine trees from the Sitgreaves National Forest were cut for the wooden vigas. Here is the west side of the building with the unfinished trade room at the top. (NPS/PEFO 26217.)

The work took nearly two years and utilized tons of stone and lumber. These photographs show the external structure nearing completion in 1938. Below, the finished building needs only to be plastered and painted. Civilian Conservation Corps crews did other projects in the monument until 1940, and when the United States entered World War II, the corps was disbanded in 1941. Many of the CCC boys enlisted and fought, becoming even bigger heroes in many different ways. The debt to this generation is substantial and worthy of honor. (Above, NPS/PEFO 20757; below, NPS/PEFO 26204.)

Six

TRAVEL ROUTES

Northern Arizona has been a travel route since prehistoric times. Following the Puerco River valley, indigenous people migrated through the grasslands, using petrified wood for building and trade. The park lies on the Hopi-Zuni Salt route. As a rite of passage, the youth of the Hopi Tribe traveled this route to retrieve salt for use on the Hopi mesas from the Zuni Salt Lake. This is depicted in this mural at the Painted Desert Inn, created by Hopi artist Fred Kabotie. (NPS/ PEFO 32846.)

The Whipple Expedition of 1853 followed the 35th parallel to lay out the first transcontinental railroad route to the Pacific Ocean. Passing through the Painted Desert area, this group was the first to document the Black Forest. In 1881, the railroad was completed through this area, making it accessible to visitors finally. Small railroad stations along the tracks provided water for steam. This photograph shows the No. 33 train pulling into the Adamana station. (NPS/JOMU 3268.024.)

The Santa Fe Railway was a big proponent of the park because destinations along the route boosted ticket sales. In the late 1800s, passengers could simply ask the conductor to let them out along the tracks to go and visit the Petrified Forest. When done visiting, the person would simply flag down the next passing train to pick them up. The railroad produced some of the first guides to the monument to promote tourism; this is the cover of the 1923 guide. (Author's collection.)

Petrified Forest, Arizona.

H. D. Co.

By the 1910s, the automobile was becoming a more popular mode of transportation; however, use of this machine required good roads for travel. Car clubs popped up across the United States, and with them came Good Roads societies. The first coast-to-coast highway was established in 1912. Called the National Old Trails Road because it followed the old pioneer and military routes, the road stretched from New York to California. The original alignment in Arizona ran from Springerville to Holbrook, passing through the southern portion of the Petrified Forest. In most places, it was not much more than a dirt track or ruts through the grass. The postcard above shows the road passing by Sphinx Rock, a prominent landmark along the road. The postcard below shows the same feature. (Above, author's collection; below, NPS/PEFO.)

SPHINX HEAD

PETRIFIED FOREST

NEAR HOLBROOK, ARIZONA

This 1923 photograph shows the National Old Trails Road route through Rainbow Canyon in the southern end of the monument. This route from Holbrook to St. Johns and Springerville started as a trail used by Mormons settling the Colorado River valley. In 1918, the State of Arizona received federal aid to improve the road. It was expanded and surfaced with gravel, and concrete dips were placed in the major wash/stream crossings. (NPS/PEFO.)

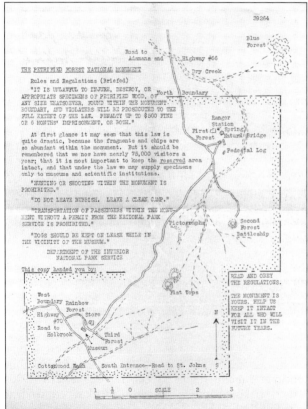

A northern branch of the National Old Trails Road (NOTR) ran from Gallup, New Mexico, to Holbrook, following the train tracks through Adamana, and was the precursor to Highway 66. This early park map shows the southern route of the NOTR (Highway 70) through the Rainbow Forest, as well as the primitive roads that ran north to south through the monument, connecting with Adamana and Highway 66 to the north. (NPS/PEFO.)

This old postcard shows the original park road running by Dick Grigsby's store in the Rainbow Forest. This building is still a gift shop today, but in the late 1920s, the store's entrance and parking area were moved to the other side of the building. (Author's collection.)

These early roads required almost continuous maintenance to remain passable. This 1920s photograph shows the park custodian (left) shaking hands with a visiting park superintendent in front of a vehicle modified for road grading. (NPS/PEFO 26296.)

In 1926, Highway 66 was officially designated. In Arizona, the northern branch of the National Old Trails Road became part of 66. At the time, there were two businesses along the road, Herbert Lore's Stone Tree House and Julia Miller's Painted Desert Park. The Painted Desert Park featured gasoline, curios, food, and a view of the Painted Desert. In this 1930s photograph, a circular sign near the gas pump shows that the spot was a Pickwick Greyhound bus stop. (NPS/PEFO 14605.)

The Painted Desert Park was more commonly called "the Lion Farm" as one of the features of the place was caged animals. This photograph, taken the same time as the one above, shows the rest of the complex, including the area where the animals were kept for exhibit. (NPS/PEFO 14626.)

This rare photograph from 1937 actually shows one of the caged mountain lions kept at the Painted Desert Park. Competition was tough between these roadside businesses, and owners were always looking for a way to get the public to stop at their place. The 1958 bypass of the Route 66 alignment doomed these businesses, and the park service purchased this place in the early 1960s. (Ball Donation, NPS/PEFO.)

In 1953, Julia Miller's son Charley Jacobs built the Painted Desert Tower trading post just down the road a few miles west of the Lion Farm. This place featured a 40-foot-tall observation tower, which, for 5¢, a visitor could climb to view the Painted Desert. This business was short lived, bypassed by Interstate 40 in 1958, and was sold to the park service around the same time. (NPS/PEFO 14617.)

Petrified Forest National Monument.. ARIZONA
Among the Fred Harvey scenic and historic locations.
Fred Harvey "3000 MILES OF HOSPITALITY" Series
See back of menu for description and further details about this series.

After World War II, the Fred Harvey Company took over operation of the Painted Desert Inn. Further interior design was done by the company's lead designer Mary Jane Colter. This included adding picture windows for views of the Painted Desert, a bright color scheme, and murals by Hopi artist Fred Kabotie. A soda fountain and dining room were added for food and other refreshments. Above is an advertisement for the Petrified Forest; the photograph below shows the soda fountain. It appears that the fountain, especially its 20¢ milkshakes and malts, was popular with children. (Above, NPS/PEFO 34116A; below, NPS/PEFO 26256.)

Originally, the Painted Desert Inn had a service garage and gasoline pumps. This structure was located where the island between the building parking lot and the main park road are today. At one point, the inn was to be the centerpiece of a new headquarters area; however, the abandonment of the nearby Route 66 alignment changed these plans, and instead, a brand-new visitors' center was built closer to the new Interstate 40. (NPS/PEFO.)

As a Harvey House, the Painted Desert Inn was home to Harvey Girls, waitresses who worked in the restaurant. Although called the Painted Desert Inn, the building never really functioned as an overnight facility. Instead, the rooms were used for boarding the Fred Harvey staff, including the Harvey Girls. Ida Logan worked at the inn as a Harvey Girl in 1942. (NPS/PEFO 35291.)

These photographs show the intersection of the main park road and Route 66. The photograph above is looking east, and below is looking west. Before the interstate, visitors would reach this intersection and turn north to see the Painted Desert or south to see the Petrified Forest. This division persists today with the misconception that there are actually two different national parks. This section was bypassed in 1958, and the asphalt was removed shortly afterwards. Today, there is a Route 66 exhibit, featuring an old car and the original telephone poles, at this location. (Above, NPS/PEFO 32200; below, NPS/PEFO 20804.)

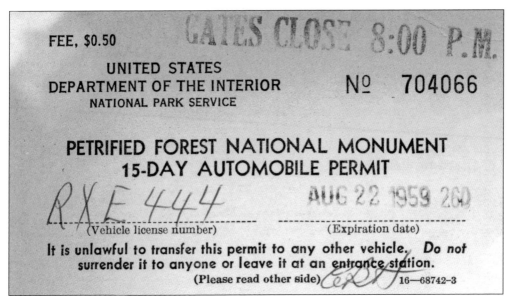

FEE, $0.50

~~GATES CLOSE 8:00 P.M.~~

UNITED STATES
DEPARTMENT OF THE INTERIOR
NATIONAL PARK SERVICE

N⁰ 704066

PETRIFIED FOREST NATIONAL MONUMENT
15-DAY AUTOMOBILE PERMIT

RXE 444

(Vehicle license number)

AUG 22 1959 260

(Expiration date)

**It is unlawful to transfer this permit to any other vehicle. Do not
surrender it to anyone or leave it at an entrance station.**
(Please read other side)   16—68742-3

In the 1940s and 1950s, visitors entering the monument would pay a fee and receive a paper pass good for 15 days. The stamp would provide the date and the entry point. "260" refers to Highway 260 at the south end of the park. (Author's collection.)

UNITED STATES DEPARTMENT OF THE INTERIOR
NATIONAL PARK SERVICE

WARNING

THE REMOVAL, DESTRUCTION,
OR CHIPPING OF PETRIFIED
WOOD IS PROHIBITED BY LAW.
PENALTY IS FINE OR IMPRIS-
ONMENT, OR BOTH.

Removal of petrified wood from the park as souvenirs had been a longtime issue. It was especially a problem along Highway 260, which carried thousands of vehicles each year and went right through one of the richest areas of petrified wood in the park. This 1958 photograph shows a ranger with one of the warning signs. In 1972, this road was rerouted outside of the park. (NPS/PEFO 18925.)

The Painted Desert Park/Lion Farm was a private inholding within the national park boundary and had long been considered a problem and an eyesore by park management. The 1955 photograph above shows a garbage dump area across from the main business. Thus, the park welcomed the 1958 Route 66 realignment to the south that became Interstate 40 later. The bypassed businesses, including the Lion Farm, tried to make the best of it but were soon abandoned and sold to the NPS. In the early 1960s, the buildings were burned and bulldozed, officially ending the Route 66 era at Petrified Forest. (Above, NPS/PEFO 24390; below, NPS/PEFO 19089.)

Seven

MISSION 66

By 1955, America's national parks were worn out with aging and insufficient infrastructure, and people began traveling the country in automobiles to see the sites. National Park Service director Conrad Wirth developed the Mission 66 program to update the parks with new infrastructure within 10 years. This early poster shows some of the ideas for a new visitors' center at the north end of the park along Route 66. (NPS/PEFO 18837.)

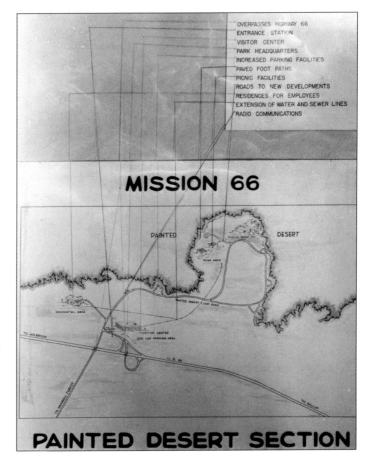

OVERPASSES HIGHWAY 66
ENTRANCE STATION
VISITOR CENTER
PARK HEADQUARTERS
INCREASED PARKING FACILITIES
PAVED FOOT PATHS
PICNIC FACILITIES
ROADS TO NEW DEVELOPMENTS
RESIDENCES FOR EMPLOYEES
EXTENSION OF WATER AND SEWER LINES
RADIO COMMUNICATIONS

MISSION 66

PAINTED DESERT SECTION

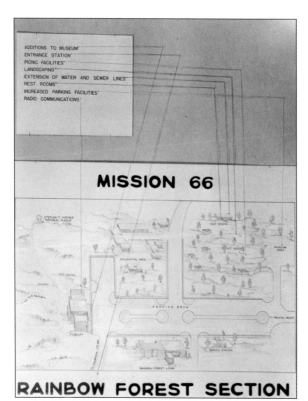

A plan was also drafted for the south end of the park, which included extensions to the visitors' center building, increased parking, and a new picnic area with restrooms. Actual changes at the south end were a new picnic structure, a shade shelter along the Long Logs Trail, and the addition of exhibit space and a sunroom on the back of the museum. (NPS/PEFO 18838.)

Other stated goals of the program were improved visitors' services, increased staff, and the removal of "unsightly structures." National park status was another stated goal. This was a display made for the Rainbow Forest Museum to explain the program and its goals to visitors. (NPS/PEFO 18839.)

The monument celebrated its 50th anniversary in 1956. Above, the National Park Service's western regional director Hugh Miller addresses the crowd at a banquet in Holbrook on December 8, 1956. Ironically, although the park's anniversary would actually have been two days before on December 6, December 8 would become important for the park in the future as this was the date when national park status was finally conferred in 1962. An anniversary would not be complete without a cake. In the photographs below is Petrified Forest National Monument's 50th birthday cake. Unfortunately, the flavors of the cake and frosting were not recorded. (Above, NPS/PEFO 15811; below, NPS/PEFO 15816.)

The overcrowded and outdated campground at Rainbow Forest in 1951 is an example of conditions in national parks that led to the Mission 66 program. Unfortunately, this campground would be closed a few years later, and as of 2020, the park still does not have a campground; however, construction is currently proceeding on one overlooking the Painted Desert. (NPS/PEFO 24963.)

The Mission 66 program supported numerous projects in the park, including road and trail improvements, the construction of shade shelters on the trails, and enhancements to the visitors' center and housing. It was the largest project program for the NPS since the CCC days before the war. This photograph shows construction of the shade shelter on the Long Logs Trail in the Rainbow Forest. (NPS/PEFO 20794.)

Other projects during this time were the expansion of the main park road to include what is now Pintado Point, the construction of the picnic area at Hózhó (previously Chinde) Point, and the naming and signage of the Painted Desert overlooks. Here is the feature sign for the Tawa Point overlook. (NPS/PEFO 18411.)

For almost 30 years, the park headquarters building at Rainbow Forest had consisted only of four rooms, one main room for visitor contact and exhibits, two smaller rooms for offices, and a basement. In 1958, the Mission 66 program funded an extension on the back of the building. This area is used for the bookstore and an expansion of the paleontology exhibits today. (NPS/PEFO 15655.)

The largest and most ambitious project was the construction of a brand new visitors' center and employee housing complex in the north end of the park, closer to Route 66. As a centerpiece of the Mission 66 program, the NPS enlisted the experienced architectural team of Robert Alexander and Richard Neutra to design the complex. It was completed and opened in 1963. This photograph shows the apartment wing of the headquarters building under construction. (NPS/PEFO 19026.)

Not only did the complex include new offices and housing for residents, it also included community areas to bring them together and, incredibly, even included an elementary school with a library and apartments for the teachers. Here is a group of students in front of the school building in the mid-1960s. (NPS/PEFO 19074.)

Building a combination workspace–residential area was ambitious for the park service at the time and reflected the Petrified Forest's status as a crown jewel of the national monuments. Neutra and Alexander designed the building to surround a central plaza reminiscent of the pueblos of local native peoples. Flat roofs exemplified the windswept plains of the area. Ribbons of glass windows and straight edges epitomized the International style of architecture. The "spider leg" steel girders in the photograph represent one of Richard Neutra's signature design elements. These photographs show construction and the newly completed plaza area. (Above, NPS/PEFO 19030; below, NPS/PEFO.)

The new visitors' center complex also included a new restaurant space for the Fred Harvey Company, which operated the park concessions at the time. The photograph above shows a portion of the diner area. A side effect of this was the abandonment of Painted Desert Inn. The late 1960s photograph of Painted Desert Inn below shows it boarded up. Note the enclosure over the old kitchen entrance on the south side of the building, showing some of the modifications that had been made in the 1950s. (Above, NPS/PEFO 18417; below, NPS/PEFO 26241.)

The new complex opened to the public in August 1963, and the open house was on August 28. The photograph above shows NPS director Conrad Wirth and park superintendent Charles Humberger leading a group of dignitaries in cutting the ribbon for the official opening. The photograph below shows the crowd in the plaza for the rest of the event. This complex was a significant expansion from the old headquarters at Rainbow Forest. (Above, NPS/PEFO 18455; below, NPS/PEFO 18459.)

The proximity of the new complex to the newly built Interstate 40 was intentional and was done to direct traffic off of the highway to visit the park. Therefore, the new visitors' center had sparse exhibits about park resources and had more regional information about the NPS. Still, it was seen as a considerable improvement over the old Rainbow Forest Museum. (NPS/PEFO 23475.)

A closing emphasis to the Mission 66 era, as well as early monument history, was the destruction of the Forest Hotel in Adamana on June 3, 1966. During a reroofing project, the building caught fire and was a complete loss. The structure that had housed so many early visitors, including John Muir, and served for nearly 20 years as the unofficial monument headquarters was no more. (NPS/PEFO 18815A.)

Eight

NATIONAL PARK STATUS

Sen. John Lacey was unsuccessful at making Petrified Forest a national park, so he used the Antiquities Act to have the area preserved as a monument. Through the 1930s, White Mountain Smith and others had also unsuccessfully lobbied for park status. By the late 1950s, the NPS supported the elevation of Petrified Forest National Monument to a national park. Finally, on March 28, 1958, Pres. Dwight D. Eisenhower signed a bill to make Petrified Forest a national park. This photograph shows a family looking at a national park map, including the new Petrified Forest National Park, in the brand-new visitors' center. (NPS/ PEFO 23480).

There was a condition to the legislation, however. National park status could not be obtained until all existing private inholdings within the park boundaries were eliminated. By 1962, there were still two private properties left, Charles Jacob's Lion Farm on old Route 66 and Olsen's Curio shop near the Puerco River. The former had been abandoned when the Route 66 alignment had been moved south to the site of present-day Interstate 40, and the property was sold. The Olsen family did not wish to sell their house and business, but in 1962, the government bought them out and moved the buildings out of the park to St. Johns. The photograph above shows an abandoned building at the Lion Farm; below is Olsen's Curio as an active business. (Above, NPS/PEFO 24383; below, NPS/PEFO 24385.)

The area of the park north of the Puerco River was grazed by cattle from the nearby Paulsell Ranch as late as 1960. This photograph shows Olsen's Curio shop and residence on the east side of the road with cattle crossing nearby. Note the prominent cattle guard across the road. This grazing was eliminated shortly after this photograph was taken, and by late 1962, the park owned all of the property within its boundaries. (NPS/PEFO 18974.)

SEPT 1960

Cartoonist Reg Manning advertised the official ceremony on October 27, 1962, with this drawing. After 200 million years, Petrified Forest was finally a national park on December 9, 1962. (NPS/PEFO 34161.)

99

Several dignitaries met at the entrance sign off Interstate 40 for the official unveiling of the new park status. Above are, from left to right, previous superintendent Fred Fageren, current superintendent Charles Humberger, and Petrified Forest Museum Association board members George L. Noel and Lloyd C. Henning. The photograph below shows the subsequent uncovering to reveal the national park title. (Above, NPS/PEFO; below NPS/PEFO 15364.)

By 1962, the park had decided to rename the main fossil forests because the existing names had become confusing. Originally named by the order in which they were reached from Adamana (First, Second, and Third), people thought those names referred to which forest had been fossilized first. So they were renamed Jasper, Crystal, and Rainbow. The Blue Forest became Blue Mesa. This is another message created by cartoonist Reg Manning asking visitors not to remove the petrified wood. (NPS/PEFO 15352.)

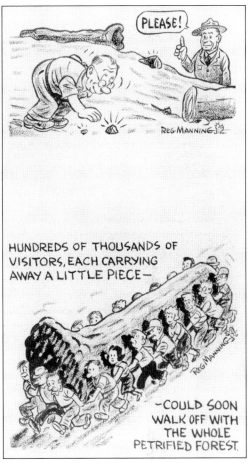

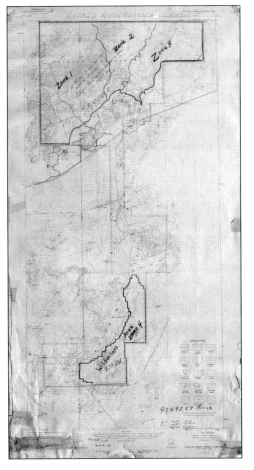

The Wilderness Act of 1964 allowed Congress to set aside and protect remaining areas of the United States that had distinctive qualities of wildness, such as no roads, buildings, or other signs of human use. Petrified Forest proposed two areas, most of the Painted Desert and the area east of Crystal Forest. This park map has the proposed wilderness areas and acreage drawn in with an approval date of October 23, 1970, one of the earliest designated wilderness areas in a national park. (NPS/PEFO 34107.)

The northern wilderness area includes the Black Forest, first documented by the Whipple Expedition in 1853. One of the largest accumulations of petrified wood in the area, it is seven million years younger than the petrified wood in the southern end of the park. That means that when the trees of the Black Forest were alive and thriving on the banks of a large river, the trees at Crystal Forest has been dead, buried, and fossilized for over seven million years. Onyx Bridge, a fossilized log undercut by a stream, partly collapsed two decades ago, but still remains a popular destination for wilderness hikers. These two 1970s photographs are from before the collapse. (Above, NPS/PEFO 32172; below, NPS/PEFO 32171.)

When new park superintendent David Ames showed up in September 1974, the Painted Desert Inn had been shuttered for more than a decade. On his desk was a demolition order for the inn that was determined to be an eyesore, especially from the newly designated wilderness area. Park ranger Jon Erickson persuaded Ames to visit the building with him; they pried off the boards and entered. Ames saw the interior work from the CCC and Mary Colter. Moved, he called up regional director Howard Chapman and asked for a reprieve from the demolition order. To save the building, they reopened it as a bicentennial wayside in 1975 and staffed it with retired NPS volunteers. The Painted Desert Inn was listed in the National Register of Historic Places the same year. The photograph above shows Ames on the left and Chapman on the right. Below is the reopened building. (Above, NPS/PEFO 23627.2; below, NPS/PEFO 26251.)

After 70 years of effort by various citizens, congressmen, and park staff, Petrified Forest was finally a national park of over 93,000 acres, revitalized by the Mission 66 program with a new headquarters complex, and with large areas of designated wilderness. The Painted Desert Inn, along with other park sites such as Puerco Pueblo, Newspaper Rock, and Agate House, had been saved and were now in the National Register of Historic Places. The park was well situated to head into the new century. These photographs show the new entrance sign and one of the new boundary signs proudly displaying national park status. (Above, NPS/PEFO 18407; below, NPS/PEFO 18406.)

Nine

THE SCIENTISTS

First and foremost, Petrified Forest is a science park, initially established to protect globally significant paleontological resources; however, archeological sites are also common and significant, as well as other historical localities and significant ecological features. The first scientists to visit were on the military expeditions that passed through in the 1850s. Lester Ward, a paleobotanist from the Smithsonian, visited in 1899, and Smithsonian archeological exploration occurred in 1901. The first vertebrate paleontology collection was made by John Muir in 1905. Muir was also enthralled with the petrified wood, as seen in this 1905 photograph. (NPS/JOMU 3268.180.)

Muir's small collection of Petrified Forest fossils ended up at the Museum of Paleontology at the University of California at Berkeley, where they were noticed by the museum benefactor, explorer, and zoologist Annie Montague Alexander. In 1921, Alexander launched a very successful expedition to look for more fossils in the Blue Forest, then just north of the monument. Joined by her partner Louise Kellogg and paleontologist Charles Camp, the group discovered numerous new fossil localities. The photograph above shows their campsite in the Blue Forest; the photograph at left shows Alexander working in the Devil's Playground area. (Both, University of California Museum of Paleontology.)

Charles Camp and his fossil preparator and field assistant Eustace Furlong returned again in 1923 and made many more significant finds. Overall, Camp's work in the Triassic of Arizona spanned several decades and his Petrified Forest work culminated in the collection of dozens of fossils and a significant published paper on the phytosaurian reptiles in 1930. The photograph above shows Charles Camp with his "machine" in the Crystal Forest in 1923; the photograph at right shows Furlong playing around in the Blue Forest the same year. (Both, University of California Museum of Paleontology.)

Early monument exhibits featured depictions and reconstructions of the animals discovered by Alexander and Camp, including this phytosaur. Phytosaurs were superficially crocodile-like reptiles common in the Triassic but only distantly related to crocodiles. Phytosaurs are still one of the most common fossils recovered in the park. (NPS/PEFO 19015.)

In 1934, the monument hired its first permanent park naturalist, Myrl Walker. He was a trained paleontologist and had worked with the Sternberg family in Kansas, well-known fossil collectors. He made discoveries of fossils throughout the Petrified Forest, including this set of phytosaur lower jaws from the Flattops area. (NPS/PEFO 15931.)

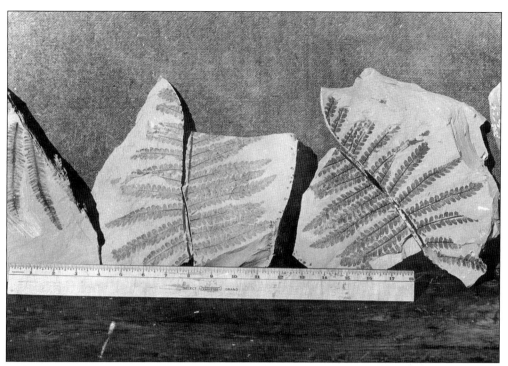

Walker also collected fossil leaves from the area, the result of the construction of the main monument road in 1932 that uncovered a horde of these fossils. The main descriptive work for the plant fossils was done by Lyman Daugherty of San Jose State. These beautiful fossil leaves, mostly from ferns, have been on exhibit in the museum since its earliest days. The photograph below is of Walker from his time at the Petrified Forest. (Above, NPS/PEFO 15549B; right, NPS/PEFO 24720.)

Walker's successor in the late 1930s was Howard Stagner, who worked to relocate and mark all of Walker's localities. Stagner also studied the local geology and noted the presence of similar fossilized leaf-bearing beds in Triassic rocks throughout Arizona. (NPS/PEFO 15573.)

Extensive archeological work was conducted by NPS archeologist Dr. Erik Reed, who performed the first comprehensive survey at the monument. Reed marked his localities with wooden posts, most of which have been rediscovered in recent years, and was the first to note the presence of a variety of archeological sites in the park, both in age and content. In this photograph, Reed looks like quite the stereotypical archeologist. (NPS/PEFO 25003.)

Archeologist H.P. Mera of the Laboratory of Anthropology of Santa Fe also worked extensively in the park prior to World War II. Mera led an extensive survey that recovered 87 more archeological sites. He also led the initial study of Puerco Pueblo and the reconstruction of Agate House, a prehistoric structure composed of petrified wood pieces. (NPS/PEFO 25005.)

In the late 1950s and early 1960s, graduate student Sidney Roy Ash started working on the fossil plants of the Petrified Forest. Completing his doctorate in 1966, Dr. Ash published several dozen papers on the park geology and fossils and worked right up to his passing in 2019. Here is Sid working in one of Walker and Daugherty's localities in the 1980s. (NPS/PEFO 24638.)

Archeologist Cal Jennings conducted more extensive excavations of Puerco Pueblo in the 1960s. The work was later filled in to protect the walls, but extensive information was collected about the site. This photograph shows a group of workers uncovering Rooms Nos. 7, 8, and 9 in 1967. (NPS/PEFO.)

In 1981, a group of paleontologists, mainly from the University of California, came back to the park to relocate Charles Camp's old fossil localities. Led by Kevin Padian and Robert Long, the group discovered dozens more sites and ushered in the current era of paleontological work. This photograph shows the group at work collecting a phytosaur skull from Cedar Tank. (NPS/PEFO 23541.)

In 1984, graduate student Bryan Small found the partial skeleton of a small dinosaur below what was then called Chinde Point. At the time, it was considered the world's most primitive dinosaur. Named *Chindesaurus bryansmalli*, it is still known almost exclusively from the Petrified Forest. This photograph shows the initial excavation work in 1984. Small is on the left. (NPS/PEFO 24580.)

The find generated extensive media coverage for the park, and to that time was the biggest vertebrate paleontology find in the park. Dinosaur skeletons are actually very rare in Triassic rocks in North America, and this one turned out to be a new species. This 1985 photograph shows the completed plastered block containing the fossil and team leader Robert Long (crouching at left) explaining the process to the press. (NPS/PEFO 24590.)

The plaster jacketed rock block containing the fossil was too large for the crew to carry up the steep slopes above the site, so a helicopter was enlisted to fly the specimen out of the Painted Desert. In the photograph above, the helicopter can be seen arriving at the site for the airlift. Dozens of media passes were issued for the event, and the coverage was fairly extensive. The photograph below, taken around the same time, shows a chance meeting at the Painted Desert Inn with Robert Long (left), Myrl Walker (center), and Sid Ash (right)—three giants of Petrified Forest paleontology. (Above, NPS/PEFO 23603.23; below, NPS/PEFO 23593.07.)

In the early 1980s, the *Chindesaurus* discovery, among others, generated a lot of excitement in the park regarding fossils. Dinosaurs were not the only fossil discoveries made by the University of California teams at that time. The photograph above shows a large phytosaur skull getting uncovered west of Lacey Point. For an exhibit, the park contracted four skeletal mounts of common Triassic animals, including a phytosaur, the rauisuchid *Postosuchus*, the aetosaur *Desmatosuchus*, and the dicynodont *Placerias*. The photograph below shows the installed phytosaur skeleton in the late 1980s. (Above, NPS/PEFO 24583; below, NPS/PEFO.)

The current paleontology program started in 2001. Since that time, hundreds of fossils have been collected, greatly enhancing people's understanding of life during the Triassic. Discoveries continue to the present day. Student interns are a big part of the work crews, where they gain invaluable experience in paleontology. The 2008 photograph above shows an intern working with paleontologist Jeffrey Martz (right), collecting a phytosaur specimen. The photograph below shows the premaxilla bone of a reptile called an azendohsaur. This find in 2014 was not only a new species for the park but also a new record for a complete family of animals. (Both, NPS/PEFO.)

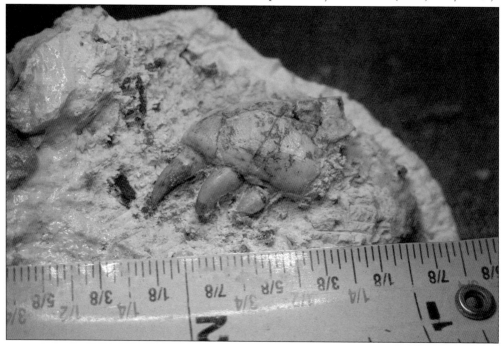

Ten

EXPANSION AND NEW FRONTIERS

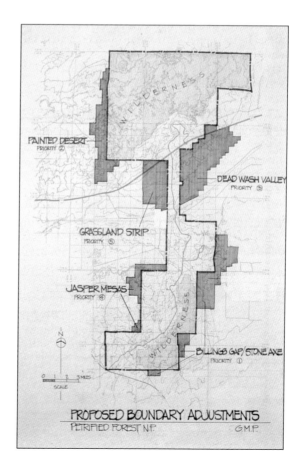

The park's 1993 General Management Plan included a section on park expansion. It has long been known that significant paleontological and archeological sites lie just outside the park boundary. There are also some important historical sites, as well as some ecological areas, that are important for protection. The initial proposal was for several important badlands exposures to the east and west, the Dead Wash petroglyphs, and the Wallace Tank Pueblo. This draft map shows the early proposed boundary. (NPS/PEFO 34697.)

117

The movement to add these lands gained steam in the early 2000s, with the National Park Conservation Association getting behind the effort. Congressional support from Arizona senators John McCain and Jon Kyl and representatives Rick Renzi and J.D. Hayworth was critical. These photographs are from a tour of the area for Congressional staffers in 2002. The photograph above is of Supt. Micki Hellickson (second from left) discussing unauthorized digging at the Wallace Tank site. The photograph below shows the group visiting the Billings Gap area. The legislation did not pass that year but was reintroduced in 2004. (Both, NPS/PEFO.)

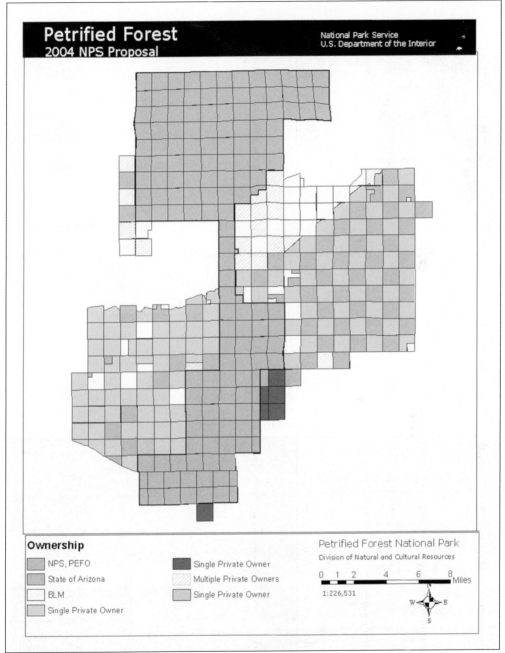

When the legislation was put forth and voted on in 2004, the map had changed numerous times in the week leading up to, and especially during the day of, the vote as the proposed acreage was debated. This map shows one version put forth in the days leading up to the vote. When the bill was finally passed, it was found that the House and Senate had voted on two different maps, voiding the passage. Thus, both the House and Senate would need to vote again, a process that can be complicated. It took another couple of days for a vote to be put forward to both chambers on the correct map. Fortunately, the bill passed again and was signed into law by Pres. George W. Bush on December 3, 2004. (NPS/PEFO.)

An event was held in honor of the passage of the expansion act. Having been instrumental in the passage of the legislation, US representative Rick Renzi from Arizona addressed the crowd. (NPS/PEFO.)

Special plaques were created and distributed to key players who had helped, including staff from the National Parks Conservation Association, the NPS Intermountain Region, and local groups like the Petrified Forest Museum Association. (NPS/PEFO.)

The final legislation added 125,000 acres to the park. Sites protected by the addition to the park include an 1870s stagecoach station with historical inscriptions, scenic badland features, and many paleontology and archeology sites. The addition of two large ranches to the east and west added acres of grasslands, which encompassed many species of plants and animals and several miles of the Puerco River riparian area. The photograph above shows an 1871 inscription from an earlier traveler along the stage route. The photograph below shows a geological area known as the "Ice Cream Rocks" because of their melted appearance. (Above, NPS/PEFO; below, Andrew Kearns, NPS/PEFO.)

Animal and geometric glyphs dominate this petroglyph panel from an area added to the park for protection. Petrified Forest contains thousands of petroglyphs scattered at sites throughout the park. (NPS/PEFO.)

As the added areas historically were large ranches in the Puerco River valley, numerous abandoned homesteads dot the landscape. At the old Paulsell Place, all that remains is the old outhouse and a long-parked Studebaker car. The ranch house itself was lost to erosion by the Puerco River years ago. (NPS/PEFO.)

In 2012, the Petrified Forest underwent a rebranding of sorts. Long known only for the petrified wood and for the illegal removal of the wood pieces by visitors, the park had actually been listed on the National Parks Conservation Association's 10 most endangered parks list in 2000 and 2001. Anecdotal stories abounded about areas being stripped clean of wood. Repeat photography of the petrified wood deposits shows little or no change through time, and in response, the park started looking to provide additional activities for visitors. One is the Pedal the Petrified annual bike event, sponsored by Northland Pioneer College. The park has also hosted a marathon and an annual orienteering event. The park provides geocaching and is very pet friendly, with its Bark Ranger program. This photograph shows one of the Pedal the Petrified participants in the Tepees around 2016. (NPS/PEFO.)

Plagued by structural problems since construction, the Painted Desert headquarters buildings were to be demolished, according to the park's 1993 General Management Plan. This decision was reversed in 2004, and the buildings were listed in the National Register of Historic Places in 2005. In 2016, they became a national historic landmark with focus on restoration back to the 1963 appearance. At the time, a major emphasis was placed on restoring the complex as close to its original appearance as possible. This included restoring covered glass, as well as the original color scheme, for the complex. The housing units and carports are being restored and returned to their original functions. The glass facade of the Painted Desert Oasis Building was completed in 2016, revitalizing the look of the plaza. (NPS/PEFO.)

In 2004, park staff started using repeat photography to look at changes in the park infrastructure and to investigate reports that the fossil wood was being removed at a significant rate. The photographs showed that the wood deposits were intact, closely resembling today what they had looked like in the past. Thus, national park protection was working, and the majority of visitors leave the petrified wood pieces in place. This set includes an original 1916 photograph of the Second (Crystal) Forest, showing not only the petrified wood but also an early shade shelter that existed there at that time. The photograph below was taken from roughly the same vantage point in 2013. The old structure has long been torn down but was added digitally to show where it had once been located. Other than the removal of the structure, hardly any differences can be seen between the photographs. (Both, NPS/PEFO.)

This set of photographs shows the Giant Logs area of Rainbow Forest, just to the east of the Old Faithful log. The photograph above is probably from the 1910s or very early 1920s because there are no buildings in the shot; the photograph below is from 2007. The Rainbow Forest Museum, associated parking lot, and employee housing are very prominent, as is the asphalt trail through the site. The main petrified wood pieces can be compared and identified, and the photograph shows that the barren areas along the trail were barren even before the trail existed. These comparisons teach park staff about rates of erosion and the effects of trail proximity on the wood deposits. (Above, NPS/PEFO; below, T. Scott Williams, NPS/PEFO.)

Another set shows the Twin Sisters logs in Crystal Forest in the 1920s and again in 2007. Portions of the closest log have been displaced, and a paved trail is present today; however, the logs themselves are mostly the same. Repeat photography is a powerful tool to show change through time and demonstrates the importance of historical photographs. Not only do these photographs record events and tell stories, they can also be used to protect special places such as national parks. (Above, Herbert Meyer Collection, NPS/PEFO; below, T. Scott Williams, NPS/PEFO.)

DISCOVER THOUSANDS OF LOCAL HISTORY BOOKS
FEATURING MILLIONS OF VINTAGE IMAGES

Arcadia Publishing, the leading local history publisher in the United States, is committed to making history accessible and meaningful through publishing books that celebrate and preserve the heritage of America's people and places.

Find more books like this at
www.arcadiapublishing.com

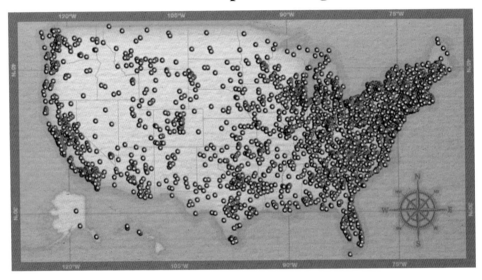

Search for your hometown history, your old stomping grounds, and even your favorite sports team.

Consistent with our mission to preserve history on a local level, this book was printed in South Carolina on American-made paper and manufactured entirely in the United States. Products carrying the accredited Forest Stewardship Council (FSC) label are printed on 100 percent FSC-certified paper.

MADE IN THE
USA